Self,

the four loves

By: H.A. HARPER

Inkwell & Pen, LLC
Conroe, Texas

SELF, POETRY SERIES

Self, Love
the four loves—
Self, Poetry Series

Copyright © 2021 – Inkwell and Pen, LLC

All rights reserved. This book is protected by the copyright laws of the United States of America. Except for brief quotations in critical publications or reviews, no part of this book may be reproduced in any manner without prior written permission from the publisher.

For contact:
inkwellandpenllc@gmail.com

For more by this author, visit
https://www.amazon.com/H-A-Harper/e/B0924W1S3Z
www.inkwellandpenllc.com

To all those longing
to love and be loved

Part 1:
An Introduction to
Self, Love

Self, Love

Shantih shantih shantih

She peers through the door

Of her makeshift shanty.

In her eyes, is the dawn,

As she smiles wildly.

Her teeth are like snow,

Shining so bright.

Her heart, purest gold.

Her skin, dark as night.

Rosy, her cheeks,

Red and lovely.

Shantih shantih shantih

Shantih shantih shantih
She appears desolate,
And yet she smiles.
Many call her poor.
She walks several miles
For work or for water;
Whatever is needed.
She's proud of herself,
Though not conceited.
The water reflects
Someone so lovely.
Shantih shantih shantih

Shantih shantih shantih
She rests in rare shade
Of her mother country;
Thinking on hard things
That leave her lonely.
But not in despair. No.
She's lonely in love,
The kind of love
That gives self up.
She loves herself,
But not herself only.
Shantih shantih shantih

Shantih shantih shantih
Under a lone shade tree,
Her prayers are emptied
For a world full of hurt
And so unforgiving.
"May they learn to love,"
Her small voice prays
To the God of her Father.
Her heart doesn't sway.
It holds fast
Without bending.
Shantih shantih shantih

Shantih shantih shantih

Too well, she knows hunger.

Too well, she knows thirst.

In her waking moment,

She was welcomed by hurt.

The world's full of weeping,

This she understands

More than most boys,

Girls, women, and men.

Still, she loves

Like her smile, wildly.

Shantih shantih shantih

Shantih shantih shantih
"How," they all ask,
"Can she smile freely?"
The answer is plain,
Though not come by easy.
She wakes on dirt floors
To face a hard day.
But when she rises up
And dusts off her face,
She has the same
Message to say,
"Self, love."
Shantih shantih shantih

Lock Up Your Heart

Deep, in the darkest, coldest pit,

There *it* can be safe. I can be certain

That the bane and blessing of it—

Love that is—will not wrap its chains

Around me. If I lock up my *heart*,

Bury it, keep it secret, hidden away,

It will not be subject to play the part

Of the victim. Unbroken, *it* will remain.

It Might be Lost

Have you not read

The right books?

Have you not watched

The right movies?

Have you not heard

The right stories?

The regrettable loss of

Something taken,

And taken for granted,

Reveals its worth.

The love that is loved

More than any,

Is the love that is lost.

What Might be Gained

Is it better to never love

Or to never lose?

If you've never loved,

You've already lost.

If you've ever lost

It is because you loved.

But love is worth the cost.

Love is what makes all,

Life itself, worth the loss.

Love is the foundation
Of all creation.
As Dante says, with all his heart,
"Love moves the sun and stars."
Love is the value that weighs
Yesterday, tomorrow, today.
And I dare say,
"Anything truly loved is never lost."
Though that loved thing is not
Eternal, in love it becomes a part
Of you, an eternal being and part
Of the Love that was before time.

What do you choose?

Never Lose?

Never Love?

Not Love At All

Neither my child nor my lover,

Neither my friend nor my enemy

Exist only in my mind—

They are not extensions of me.

If I love myself more,

I will not love them more.

If I love myself more,

I will put myself before

Whatever they need.

This is not love at all.

This is the source of all

Hate.

Now, that is Love

Neither my child nor my lover,

Neither my friend nor my enemy

Were made for me;

Rather, I was made for them.

I was made to lift them up.

I was made to love them.

I was made to esteem them more.

I was made to cherish them.

Simulated Love

Storge

Without explanation.

Without reason.

Without being told.

Without 1s and 0s.

Natural.

When a child embraces a mother,

When a mother forgives a child,

When a brother protects a sister,

When a sister protects a brother,

When siblings give up a right

To appease the other,

This is love.

The smiles at family gatherings,

A grandparent's present of bribery,

A great-grandmother's pinch on the cheek,

This cannot be, actually, simulated.

Eros

To taste. To touch.

To feel what is real

Running through my fingertips.

The warmth of skin,

Friction, against skin.

The passion of lips

Pressed against lips.

A real pleasure. Not simulated.

There is nothing like it.

Philia

That connection between two souls,

Where some common ground leads

Each to lay themselves down,

To look past the partition of self

And embrace, with a treasured part

Of their soul never revealed

Before, for one another.

Can this be bottled up,

Quantified, dematerialized?

In our hearts we cry,

And our cry is justified,

No!

Agape

Can the creator,

Will the creator

Lower themselves,

Humble themselves

To be weak like the

Creation to redeem,

In love, those hurting

And lost in search of hope?

Will they feel pain?

Real, true pain

And die? Actually die

And conquer the death,

The flatline that comes

When all is unplugged?

What's Good?

The good lover shares something

With the good friend.

The good friend shares something

With the good child.

The lover, the friend, and the child

All share something.

They are good.

Love Defined

Can anyone really define love?
Is it just a word subjected to one's
Limited vocabulary, limited mind?
Is love a word of that kind?
Maybe it is more than a word.
Maybe it is more than can be heard
When the oft spoken phrase
Moves from one's lips, reverberates,
To another's ears.

Can love be boxed up neatly

in a sentence or two, completely?

Can letters and corresponding sounds

Provide a person with the right ground

To express that emotion so profound,

To trust that reality beyond solid ground,

To live out that natural state

Not subjected to fate,

Although it is destined?

Do you want love defined?
Do you want it confined
To one crafty sentence?
I do not—and for good reason.
Love defined
Is too much for one lifetime.
Love is eternal. Love is action.
It is not limited to passion.
It is not limited to blood.
Love is everyone
Moving together as one.
And still, love is more:
Love is three persons—
Three holy persons—
Who are, have been,
And will always be,
Without end,
One.

Love Declared

As yourself . . .
(Comme toi meme)
Speak to the soul:
To the whole being—
To the body and the mind, too.

Speak of love lost.
Speak of love gained.
Speak of sacrifice.
Speak of the reign
Of never ending kingdoms
Whose foundations
Are of old, of everlasting.

Write of those not invented.
Write of those discovered.
Write of those who lay
Themselves down
For their lover,
Those who go
To the breach
For their brother,
Those who face hell
For their enemy.

Declare something
Beyond life
In your story . . .
(le mythe de l'amour)

Part 1:
Affection —
Self, Storge

Affection

I rise early.

The smell of coffee beans roasting

Permeates the morning air.

I inhale the refreshing smell

Of medium roast.

I hear the popping toast.

I pop out of bed.

I open the door

And jettison down the hallway.

The ting of pans

And utensils lightly clash—

Ringing in the new day.

They dance together

Their familiar dance.

Mix. Flip. Whip
A filling breakfast into shape.
I step into the doorway
And see an angel
At her morning toil:
Preparing all a filling meal
That will steal away the yet felt
Sorrows of the day.

"Mom," I say.

She does not turn.

She points at the platters

Brimming with affection.

I am overwhelmed.

Not because this is new.

No. But because it makes me new

Every morning.

Her work is consistently

Without complaint.

Her affection is balanced—

It is give and take.

She demands, as she gives,

Without hesitation.

She loves without reservation:

A firm-handed love.

It is an art. A true art,

Like a sweet confection,

Her undying affection.

Her art plays its part

On every breakfast plate,

In every full heart and belly.

I sit to take part in this art.

I fill my plate. I begin to taste.

This is love. This is affection.

The Grind

6:00 a.m.

Kisses. Hugs.

Out the door.

Fight traffic.

Lift. Sweat.

Muscles ache.

Bones strain.

Break.

Bend. Lift.

Twist. Crouch.

Working fingers

To the bone.

Fight traffic.

In the door.

Kisses. Hugs.

6:00 p.m.

Repeat.

Why?

Why does he do it?

How?

How does he do it?

Again.

Again.

Over.

Over.

The monotony.

The stress.

Did he have dreams?

Did he have hopes?

Is this what he always wanted?

Yes. Yes. Yes.

He is a father

And this is what is required,

This is a part of everything

He deems precious—

The kisses and hugs.

Storge: Self-Love

With aching chest, with a strain in my breast,

I look upon the downcast soul, aghast.

What are these tears I see? What is her pain?

I sympathize, though unaware the strain.

The downcast soul turns sobs to a blue sky:
"Why'd you take my love? He was mine? ALL MINE."
Reply? Listen. Not one. She sits, waiting,
With photo in her hand—photo, fading.

Its content is clearly an infant boy

Playing with his prized and precious stuffed toy.

Another comes to comfort this mother.

The other must be the young boy's father.

A sudden shift in countenance. Anger foams,
"Back! You cannot know! He was mine, alone!"
But what she could not see within this man
Was a dark pain no man could understand,
> Save for this woman.

Love is NOT Enough … Well …

Love is not enough.

Well, not that kind of love …

Not when it is on its own.

Affection, I mean.

That kind of love:

Affection without self-control,

Affection without mercy,

Affection without sense,

Affection that is just sensation

Is not enough.

Successful Storge

When tested, she realized
That though she had
Always *loved* this child,
This blood of her blood,
She had never *loved* them
More than what was natural.
Maybe she had never *loved*
That child more than
> The mother bird *loves*
> Her chicks
> Or the mother dog *loves*
> Her pups.
> But now, her *love* has
> Been tested.
> And in the test she has
> Come to have a true
> Affection.
> The real goal of natural
> *Love*.

What is More Powerful

Do you remember the times,

Back when we were just kids,

When we would run and play,

When we would laugh all day,

When our greatest hope

Was being together?

Nothing was better.

Nothing was better.

I do.

I do remember.

I thought that was life.

I thought that was living.

I thought that was special.

Was I wrong?

Just the other day, I was reminiscing about…

You know how I love to do that.

I am so sentimental. Anyway, I…

No, wait. You don't know.

You don't know me anymore.

We are barely less than strangers

When we must shake hands at the door

Or share an affectionate hug.

Sure, we put on a good show

On those rare occasions

When we do pretend things are

Just as they once were.

But they are not.

Do I know you? I am afraid not.

All my life, I thought I knew.

I guess I was wrong.

I was certain. So certain.

Now I see, I played the fool.

What is more powerful, Love or Death?

You say love. So did I, once.

No longer. I see what death has done.

That cloaked, old skeleton is tough.

He makes his cuts rough and splits

The heart, the mind, the soul,

The Family in two, three,

Or whatever is necessary

To fill the grave with despair

That spills over into life.

You can play the fool, if you want.

I do not want to anymore.

I will have love,

But not like it was.

I will have love

That is truly balanced.

Love that is of a kind

That is not ruled by

Shallow necessity.

Rather, love that is ruled by

Love in its purity:

Perfect love. Godly love.

Love that does not bend

Because of the circumstance.

What we had when we were young,

It was love … it was love.

There is no doubt in my mind.

But that kind of love

Cannot stand on its own.

At least, it cannot stand

In the wake of death.

It is swept away with the undertow.

I don't know what to do.

I don't know what can be done.

If we are to go on in love,

It must be renewed.

Those times I remember,

Must be baptized.

I never thought that death

Would reveal our affection

To be nothing but pretension

That relied solely on that one

Or two who held it all together.

I don't understand why death

Hasn't brought us together,

Stronger than ever.

I don't. It just hasn't.

Our love, our affection

Was just not enough.

The Prayer of a Father

O Sweet Lord, lead her to be

Ever kind and most friendly

To those who love to see

Her smiling face grace the day.

O Sweet Lord, give her strength

To do right by those watching in length:

Her ups and downs and all arounds;

Her lovely face that graces the day.

O Sweet Lord, she trusts in you.

Call her loving heart to do

What she must to please you,

To see your lovely face, grace her day.

Close

The sweet smell of

A first breath.

The warmth of

A first touch.

The pain of

A first kiss.

Hold her close.

The breaking joy of
A first smile.
The peace of
A first laugh.
The loss of
A first cry.
Hold him close.

In life, there are many firsts.
In life, there are many joys.
In life, there are many loves.
In life, there are many losses.
No one can be shielded forever.
Nevertheless, not to shield,
Only to strengthen,
Hold them close.

FATHER

From that first cry heard in the hospital,

And the moment later when a desperate, frail body appears,

Trembling with unknowable, unspeakable emotions,

His heart is hooked.

Everything has changed—it is no longer about "me"; now there is someone else.

Ready or not, life has begun—he has been born again.

SON

Saying what it means to be the son of a mother—

O' precious as a golden sun the morning after a cold, devastating night—

and a father whose very presence is a strength that tames the uncertain seas of life, is . . .

Nearly impossible.

BROTHERS

Before birth, we were destined to something more
> than can ever be expressed in words.

Real is the word; if there even is one. Something real…
> HONEST… not faked. It can't be undone.

Ordinary as it is (common, I mean), it is extraordinary
> that two, so much the same, and yet so different,
> would be bound by destiny, bound by blood.

Then again, it is more than destiny, it is more than
> words, blood, time, can define. It is…

Empty is my mouth when I try to say it. It can only be
> lived in love with a laughter no one can know,
> save for us two—perpetually, an inside joke.

Really, though, it is no joke at all.

Seriously.

SISTERS

Soon they became

Inseparable, like a mirror and the image

        it reflects. Like the

Sun and its dawn,

The one could not be, fully, herself without

        the other. Never could

Either come to

Realize a world that was possible without

        their companion, their friend, their

Sister.

MOTHER

Mending is the power

Of her kiss, hug,

Tears, and never ceasing prayer.

Healing is the listening

Ear—a treasure from God above.

Ready, at any moment, to fix you.

Molding

What they gave me,

That natural affection

Born in blood,

Are the very best

Parts of me.

Yes, if there is, indeed,

Anything good,

Anything honorable,

Anything lovely in me,

It was produced

By the molding

Of their love.

Roots

The roots anchor into soil
Thicker than blood,
Though watered by it.

The branches reach into
Past, Present, and Yet-to-come
Without hindrance.

The trunk is like iron:
It withstands the flood,
Though affected by it.

It stands. It grows.
It reaches out through time,
Connecting many
In one blood,
In one soil,
In one tree,
In one family.

Natural

Lonely child, wherever you are,

You do not deserve your plight.

It's only natural to seek a mother's care;

It is, by birth, an inalienable right

To be loved by father and mother alike.

Dear mother, alone in your years,
You are worth more than the tears
That seem to be your only companion.
You should be honored by children.
You should be surrounded by love.

Father, you worked fingers to bone,
You sold all your dreams in hopes
That your children would be blessed,
That they would be your second chance
At doing something right in this life.

The care a child deserves and yearns,
The love a mother longs for in return,
The sacrifice that makes a father stern
Are all natural desires of human-beings—
The natural love and affection they need.

Breathing Helps

"Take a breath. Take a breath.
It hurt to watch them go,
But now they're gone."

"Where did they go and
Are they gone for good?
Are they gone for evil?
Can their new journey be understood?
Is this goodbye…farewell…so long, forever?
Adieu…Adieu…Will I ever see you again?
To God…To God…I hope you go and then
I hope I follow…Will I attain my hope?
Can I ever surely know in this life
Or must I, too, die and be bid
Adieu…Adieu?"

"Take a breath. Take a breath. Breathing helps."

Part 2:

Passion —

Self, Eros

A Lover's Last Words

It is late. I've barely slept in days.

How can I at a time like this?

It's hard to believe this is happening.

And yet, it is. I can't stop this.

All your life, you imagine such days.

But when they come, it's not the same.

The clock ticks slow.

The night lingers on.

As I sit here and watch him breathe,
His chest slowly sinking and rising,
My mind wanders in dazed sleep.
I think on the past. The time creeps
by, the time of moments long past,
Before this chair, this place where I sit
And wait to see
No more, he breathes.

A brisk whisper breaks my foggy daze.
This word I've heard his voice say
So many times before. But never like this.
"Honey," he beckons me to his side
With all the might he has left inside—
Nothing more than a faint crack of breath.
I rise and step
Up to his bed.

He is smiling. His eyes, half open.
"What is it?" I ask. He says nothing.
He smiles. Only a smile. A pacific smile.
I lean over. I place my wrinkled hands
Under his grey, wooly head. So fragile.
With the sweetest voice I can muster,
I try to give him, and myself,
A word of comfort.

As if I was just that same young girl
That he fell in love with a lifetime ago,
I ask this lover of mine, "Do you know
how you're going to know it's me when
We meet in heaven?" He holds his grin.
Not a word crosses his lips. I continue,
"I'm going to say,
'Hello, Darlin'.'"

I smile back, though his eyes are shut,
Hoping my words received, conscious.
No response. Does he hear me? He must
Smile because he knows I am here and
He no longer has the strength to speak
anymore. I…

His lips begin to move.
He murmurs with cracked voice,
"Hello, Darlin'."

I lean in. I gently press my lips to his.
A dainty tear slips from my cheek to his.
I lay his head down. While I still caress
The back of his head with my left hand,
I thumb away my tear from his aged cheek
with my right. I inhale and exhale slowly
As I cozy back
Into my chair.

I look down at the Bible on the table
Next to me. I think about eternity.
I think about our life together. I think
until…
I wake.
I must've dozed off. I look up in a daze.
I stare at his chest, waiting to see if… if…
Does it rise and fall? Does he breathe at all?
Not a movement appears. A rush of fear
Burns my cheeks. I am now fully awake,
though frozen in place.
I know the truth.

I sit forward in my chair and I…
I try to stand. My legs shake. I…
I know I can't. I lean back and
Breathe. My eyes locked on his face,
A face once full of life, wisdom,
love, passion, and so much more
is now so…
I don't know.

Tears well up in my eyes, then trickle
Down to my breast. A lump strangles
My throat. I try to push it past and speak
My last words, in this life, to the being
With whom I fully, truly, honestly loved
And shared this life. My jaw is quivering.
Heartbroken, I say,
"Goodbye, Darlin'."

In Death We Do Not Part

In the pouring rain,

Your smile is just in sight.

I catch you in my arms.

It's moments like tonight

That tell me:

When I'm standing up
On the streets of gold,
At the gates of heaven,
You'll be holding my hand,
And we'll finally see
We've made it together—
In death we do not part.

In the calm of the storm
We are miles apart,
And I'm dreaming of you—
Dreaming of that moment
When I'll see you . . .

When I'm standing up
On the streets of gold,
At the gates of heaven,
You'll be holding my hand,
And we'll finally see
We've made it together—
In death we do not part.

We've made it, baby.

We've made it!

And together we'll hear:

"Well done, my beautiful ones."

Half-Smile

All of the tension rising from that half-smile

you give me keeps me convinced

that every nerve-racking second of this means

much more to me than anything.

You're beautiful eyes are what

keep me moving on.

Out for the Count

Short of glory like a Seattle sunrise,

Burning for your mercy.

Drowning in your memories.

Like a hopeless paradise,

It's coming around again.

You don't notice

You can't stop this.

You don't notice

You can't stop this.

We're gonna make it better.

We could never stop here.

So end this conversation.

End this conversation, right now.

Don't you see that they can't stop us?

Don't you see that no one can stop us?

We'll fight this fog till the morning comes.

We'll fight this Seattle sunrise.

Will it come with the morning
Or melt with the break of day?
Will we fight our way to the end?
Or maybe tonight is too late.

You don't notice
You can't stop this.
You don't notice
You can't stop this.

We're gonna make it better.

We could never stop here.

So end this conversation.

End this conversation, right now.

Don't you see that they can't stop us?

Don't you see that no one can stop us?

We'll fight this fog till the morning comes.

We'll fight this Seattle sunrise.

Simple but True

This is beautiful just like your face,
Just like your eyes.
It's worth more than I can say,
Even if I say it twice.

I know you like it this way,
Even though it's simple at times.
And I lose it all again
Just to say this twice.

You like it this way, you…

Would you write this for me too?
If I did not write this for
You?
And would you say this for me too?
And would you say this again?

This is beautiful just like your face,
Just like your eyes.
It's worth more than I can say,
Even if I say it twice.

I know you like it this way,
Even though it's simple at times.
And I lose it all again
Just to say this twice.

You like it this way.
You like it this way.

You like it this way.
You like it this way.

You…

Would you write this for me too?

If I did not write this for

You?

And would you say this for me too?

And would you say this again?

And would you say this again?

A Picture Isn't Enough

A picture isn't enough

To settle this restless heart.

A dream could never be this true.

We played our games

And we played them smart.

Spoil me in thoughts of you.

I thought I told you,

But I guess you didn't listen:

"We are meant to be

And nothing is missing."

Perfect in beauty and style.

I beg your presence just a little while.

All I ask is for your love.

Tell me what you need.

A thousand words

And not a single empty phrase in it.

So many love letters,

But who kept count anyway.

It's overbearing,

But just not enough.

I speak your name in the dark of night.

I speak your name.

Your childish looks.

The endless stares.

My soft lips pressed to yours.

A picture isn't enough

To settle this restless heart.

A dream could never be this true.

We played our games

And we played them smart.

Spoil me in thoughts of you.

The Sun and the Other Stars

There was a time when,

I swear it, I thought moving

The sun and the other stars

Just to feel you close,

Just to feel your heart,

Would have been

A task worthy of its end.

There was a time when,
I see now, I was wrong.
When love was limited
By the lie of time.

But now I see clearly:

Our love cannot be whole

On its own;

There is a greater love

That moves

The sun and the other stars.

Only in the light of that love

Can our love stand

The test of time.

Only in the light of *the* Love

That truly moves the sun

And the other stars

Can our love,

Can any love,

Be true.

A Passing Fancy

One fine autumn day, while a chill lingered in the air,

One of those leafy breezes that sweep past feet

With dusty twirls and flip through curls of hair,

I strolled down the sidewalk by an Italian restaurant

Listening to my dear friends talk that pointless talk,

Filled with banter and laughter, about our wasted youth.

And as I walked and talked, I locked onto a beauty

Who sauntered down the walk across the street,

Moving my heart to beat with such rapidity

That, for what felt an eternity, I stopped and stared—

My eyes were foolishly, incautiously, caught up

(No! Called up and away!) from their wasted state:

Finding their purpose at last; the reason they opened

On that fair day after coming out of the womb.

Then, to my surprise, that beauty with green eyes

Stopped quick, halting in their path, to stare back.

At first sight, I knew our heartbeats entwined.

Fever flushed my cheeks; then sank to knock my knees.

I could see, those eyes could see we felt the same

Rush and blush—stricken by this love that came

So easily, so naturally, so quickly . . . and then . . .

With nothing but a half-smile and awkward wave,

Both of us, never looking back, went on our way.

Yet something tells me, neither will ever be the same.

Face to Face

How beautiful it is when two souls meet
In the throes of self-less embrace,
Face to face.

Eros: Self-Love

There once was a man

Whose love was found

In a silvery pool,

Resting on the ground

Of a darkening wood.

Two lovers were bound

To meet face to face

With an echoing sound

Of cursed, scorned love—

Unrequited: Profound.

When met lovers' eyes

In the watery glass,

Something caught hold

With a wicked grasp

That wouldn't let go,

That wouldn't relent,

That wouldn't kiss back

Yearning young lips—

A curse had been sent

On this unrepentant.

So stared the man

Into the cool pond

Until withered down,

All traces were gone—

Nothing left of the fool

Save for this one gem:

Six petals, one cup

Atop a green stem,

A flower; that's all

That was left of him.

YOU ARE MINE

The way you make me feel,

The burning passion inside,

I will have . . . I will take you.

You are mine. You ARE mine.

YOU are Mine . . .

A deep obsession twisting thought.

A mark I'm not to cross, a line

That means nothing. You can't stop me.

You are mine. You are MINE.

YOU ARE MINE . . .

You are mine.

The pounding in my chest hurts.

There is one cure I have in mind.

I'll take all of you. You can't stop me.

You are mine. You are mine

You ARE MINE . . .

YOU ARE MINE

Youaremine Youaremine Youaremine Youaremine
Youaremine Youaremine Youaremine Youaremine
Youaremine Youaremine Youaremine Youaremine
Youaremine Youaremine Youaremine Youaremine
Youaremine Youaremine Youaremine Youaremine
Youaremine Youaremine Youaremine Youaremine
Youaremine Youaremine Youaremine Youaremine
Youaremine Youaremine Youaremine Youaremine
Youaremine Youaremine Youaremine Youaremine
Youaremine Youaremine Youaremine Youaremine
Youaremine Youaremine Youaremine Youaremine
Youaremine Youaremine Youaremine Youaremine
Youaremine Youaremine Youaremine Youaremine
Youaremine Youaremine Youaremine Youaremine
Youaremine Youaremine Youaremine Youaremine
Youaremine Youaremine Youaremine Youaremine
Youaremine Youaremine Youaremine Youaremine
Youaremine Youaremine Youaremine Youaremine
Youaremine Youaremine Youaremine Youaremine

The Bond of Unity

Imagine, if you will,

A world in which

The most sure sign

And expression of Eros,

What is supposed to be

A special bond of unity

Where two bodies meet,

Two desperate souls physically

Come together as one

In a world undone

By selfish pride,

Is consumed

Without regard,

Selfishly—

As if it's nothing more

Than a cheap dessert.

More than Conquerors

What's the matter angel?

Can't you speak out in defense

Or give a tasteless phrase of conflict?

The sweet smell of a one night stand

And the slick one-liners your bright eyes demand.

Admit it: you forgot my name,

Or chose to release the relentless shame.

The water runs down my neck in blistering heat.

So, I pray for a sign but expect defeat.

I let you take my future, complicate my desires.

I'll have you know your position is dire.

I surrender.

I'm afraid you've gone too far
For us to come back.
I'm afraid it's gone too far to
Turn around (kiss me goodbye).
I'm afraid it's already done.
I put my finger to your lips
As you hear my goodbye.

And as I walk away,
I hear you say,
"I surrender."

To Bake a Cake

There once was a baker who baked

The most extravagant of cakes:

Ten foot high, six foot wide,

Layer upon Layer;

Oh, and the colors,

Many hues did coincide.

Days upon days, they took to bake.

What beautiful creations were made.

And once all was done,

Every inch, PERFECTION,

(this lovely confection)

All would come see—

No touching, nor tasting:

Looking, 'loving'

(If that's what that means).

Once the show was over,

The baker would take

The creation baked

And throw it away.

All would say,

"What a waste,"

Then line up the next viewing day.

Asking for a Friend

When a Queen flaunts the ring
Of her inheritance, when she flings
It about and wields it carelessly,
Is that considered empowering?
It seems the power is in the ring,
No matter how one wears the thing.
The question should be, then, how
Should the Queen wield such power?
If she loves this precious gift,
The sign and right of inheritance,
If she loves herself at all,
If she gives the gift regard,
Shouldn't she respect her power?
Shouldn't she reserve it for the hour
Ordained by One greater than all,
An hour when her power will fall
Subject to a most empowering thing,
When two become one in matrimony?
Asking for a friend.

Part 3:
Friendship —
Self, Philia

More than Friends . . . Lovers

Two become one

In a perfect bond

Of unity.

And soon that love grows

To a worth unknown

That far exceeds

The passion and lust, the heat of

The moment, the overwhelming rush

of Eros.

More than first sight,

More than a fairytale,

More than 'Once upon a time…',

More than most stories ever tell

Is the love

That grows beyond

Its beginning to combine

Two selves as one

In the form of many loves.

By My Side

I know it is not easy to stay.

I think I know the effort it takes

To stay by my side.

I am arrogant in this,

But I am not truly sorry.

I am a fallen creature

Defined by foolish pride.

I do not make it easy,
At least I know that.
By this knowledge
I, full of pride, boast.
I do not think I could
Stand by me, as you have
Done faithfully, my host.
Through all that I have done,
Through all that I have said,
You continue to host me
When my sins leave me
In deserved death.

Word and deed,

You hold steady.

Word and deed,

I do not.

You are

A true companion

To a fool

That deserves you not.

You Too?

What delight! You too?

For, oh, so long I knew

I was the one, only true

Lover of this special tune.

But now I know there's two

And we need never lose

The delight of our new

And precious friendship.

The Meeting

Two childhood friends
Were sent far from home,
To a land of bullets and bombs.
Separated in this land,
Both knowing not
Whether the other was dead,
They looked to the sky,
Prayed and begged
That one day they'd
Be united again.

Unlike many young men,

These two friends

Found their way home

To that small town

They'd always known.

There their friendship

Grew with another bond—

A bond beyond childhood.

These two understood

A hurt so few could.

But as young men should,

They grew older.

And as friends shouldn't,

They grew apart.

Not that they ceased

To be dear friends;

Their jobs played this part.

One moved to the east.

The other to the west.

Then time played its part.

For 46 years they wrote.

But allow, life did not,

For the two to meet—

Each got married,

Had kids, and grew old—

Until today. Today is the day,

Like all those years ago,

The two will come home

And unite again,

The dearest friends.

Self-Love: Philia

As you sit quietly,

I continue to speak,

As usual, about me.

Wait patiently.

I will allow you to speak,

If what you speak

Is about me,

If what you speak

Is good to me.

Speak up. Speak up.
My patience wears thin.
Don't go on in silence,
Neglecting to lift me up,
Forgetting to bask in
The blessing I give
With my presence.
I want—I need—I must,
And you must give in.

Sacrifice yourself
For our relationship.
You should, you know.
It's for your own good.
My needs must be met:
I must come first.
That's how this works:
What we have, that is—
This self-love friendship.

More

Views. Shares. Follows. Likes.
These are not friendship.
These are nothing like
What friendship means.
These take no sacrifice
Other than the moment in time,
Given with little more
Than a fleeting whim.

Friendship is not about me.
Friendship is more than a screen
Balanced in my hand.
Friendship is more than me.
Friendship is more than one.
Friendship is a relationship.
Friendship is not about benefit.
Friendship costs.

Not money. No. That is cheap.

The price one pays,

Or should be willing to pay,

For their friend

Is far too high a price

For money to buy.

Friendship is

A life for a life.

Which Never Fades

Though years pass,
Long years that are not
Blessed with your presence,
There is something special
That we share, something
Which never fades.

Every time I, again,
See your face, your smile,
I am taken back to
Another time, another life—
A place long gone, though
Still alive in my heart.

Sit With Me

Sit with me. Don't speak a word.
What I need is just to be heard,
Not understood, not chastised.
All I need is someone by my side
To hold me tight and let me know,
In the darkest night of my soul,
With nothing but their presence,
"In the end, there will be peace."
Sit with me. All I need is a friend.

Feed My Sheep

Do you love me?

Do you love me?

Do you love me?

Three times he spoke,

For he had to know

If his friend would

Hold out to the end.

Do you love me?
Do you love me?
Do you love me?
Three times he spoke
And broke his friend's
Heart—a fragile soul,
Broken by Love's toll.

Do you love me?

Do you love me?

Do you love me?

With assurance of tears,

This friend of long years

Gave his reply—steady, true—

"Lord, you know I love you."

The Promise

Two friends make a promise
Only one may have to keep.
Soon, rockets will burst and
Mud will flow up to the knee,
Mixed with the blood of enemies.

The smoke will rise high
Above dead and dying men.
Amongst those men will be
A promise making friend—
For victory, a life is given.

Tested will be the one
Left to fulfill the promise.
It will be his to choose:
Be foul or be honest—
The other promiser will be dead.

If this promise is in love,
The promise will be kept
Above all benefit to the one
Friend left to keep the promise.
It will be his promise to keep.

Two friends make a promise

Only one will keep.

It Doesn't Make Sense

Think back through eons,

Look deep into the past,

Then it may be realized,

You may come to it at last,

That giving one's life

For the sake of their friend

Is of no earthly benefit to them—

no-no-no-no—

It doesn't make sense.

And yet, in our heart of hearts,
At the foundation of our soul,
we know-we know-we know- we know,
Giving one's life for their friend
Is the right thing to do, in the end.

Lifelong: Evergreen

Their leaves never fade

From their native colors,

From their lively hue

To dingy earthen tones.

Nor do they fall into

Patterns of reds and yellows.

The years have no say.

The seasons have no power.

Nothing can separate them

From the glory of their crown.

The Hero from Bagshot Row

There is a friend, closer than a brother;
Through thick and thin, you'll wish for no other.

His comfort, sweet; yes, sweeter than honey:
His care, like lembas, keeps for long journeys.

Look past his stature, for value's unseen:
Look in his heart, there is treasure beneath.

He may appear to be boorish and coarse;
But on his shoulder, he'll bear up your course.

Tempered, tested—much more precious than gold:
His glitter is his soul, this dear *mellon*.

Part 4:
Godly —
Self, Agape

God, the Playwright

Tragedy

>Blood & water. Blood & sweat.

>Gall & vinegar. Sin & debt.

God, your God has forsaken you.

Friend, your Friends have abandoned you.

Groom, your Bride has forgotten you.

Son, your Mother is watching you.

>Give up the Ghost. Give up your Mother.

>Destined to die. Destined to suffer.

'how are the mighty fallen!'

>(2 Samuel 1:27)

Comedy

    Begotten & God. Dead & risen.

    Rich & poor. Giver & given.

Stable, I AM is born in you.

Colt, the King is riding you.

Cross, the Savior is hung on you.

Grave, the Life is buried in you.

    The blind do see and the seeing are blind.

    Eternity has stepped into time.

'the foolishness of God

is wiser than men.'

    (1 Corinthians 1:25)

Fairy Tale

    Serpent & fruit. Guilt & flood.

    Grace & Truth. Mercy & love.

Accuser, the Truth accuses you.

Dragon, the Knight comes for you.

Hell, the Way cuts through you.

Death, the Victor overthrows you.

    Sing! you guests to the Holy One;

    At the ageless dance in the age to come.

'behold, I am alive

for evermore, Amen.'

    (Revelation 1:18)

God is Love

God is Love and Love never ends:
But with kith and kin, it does bend
And, sometimes, it will break.

God is Love and Love is the call:
The call that falls upon us all,
Even those who forsake.

God is Love and Love is the end:
The end of breaks that need to mend—
Forgive for heaven's sake!

God is Love; Love never began—
It begins all that does not end;
Except, it ends the break.

God is Love and Love's in the air.
God's love brings a time of cheer.
Imagine what's at stake.

God is Love and Love is present:
Give thanks. Give grace. Yes, repent.
Love is all it will take.

Reason Knows Nothing About

By the spoken word, the cosmos were formed:

The ineffable mysteries of the universe cascading about
    in distances surpassing comprehension;
The possible yet-to-be-discovered sentient beings
    romping and lazing in the cordial warmth of a
    distant sun at the center of an unknown galaxy;
The stardust trailing the souls of long deceased and
    forgotten beings as they break through the
    atmosphere which have encouraged the hopeful
    words gracing the wishes of so many children;
The seeds of bright stars drifting near the edge of that
    final sphere, seeds whose very elements have
    tasted the lips of God.

And yet, without the vibration of a single syllable touching my ears,
Before I was old enough to know reason or logic, or differentiate sound,
An intuited truth pervaded every inch of my being.

When I was nothing more than an innocent child, my heart knew,
Yearned for, trusted that there is more to life than uncertain chance,
Than science and circumstance.

Before such words meant anything at all, I knew, I felt, my imagination
Assured me that at the center of all is something more—
Beyond reason, logic, and facts is the source: the Love that moves all.
The Love that I, and all sane beings, crave.

Can't Stop Now

Father, soothe me with your voice.

Let my every waking moment

Be in your arms.

Lift me up and pull me out.

I've grown tired of fighting.

Carry me far from here.

I can't make it on my own.

Cover my eyes from this firefight.

I can't make it.

I can't find the strength
To lift my hands
And praise your name.
You are so wonderful,
And graceful is your presence.
Carry me far from here.

I can't make it on my own.
Cover my eyes from this firefight.

You've lifted me up.
I'm singing your name
And I can't stop,
I can't stop now.
You gave me hope.
You know I've changed.
Father, you can't stop,
You can't stop now.

Derelict

Naked shame.

Vitriol disdain.

Violent words

Hurled in vain.

    Children throw rocks,

    Grandmothers thumb their nose,

    Soldiers mock,

    Criminals expel bitter prose

    Against this one whose blood flows

    Redder than the red, red rose.

In pain,

He cries.

Derelict,

He cries:

> "Why? Why? Why?
>
> My God, my Father, why?
>
> Why have you forsaken me?
>
> Why have you led me to die?"

With quaking earth,

Breaking rocks,

Opening tombs,

Renting veil in two,

> His God, his Father replies.
> His God, his Father tells him why—
> Why he lived and now must die
> The forsaken death he will die.

"Love."

E. N. E. M. Y.

Even if it hurts my pride,
No matter, I must decide to
Extinguish the flame of burning hate.
My heart, my mind, my soul, the weight
Yanks me down to eternal sorrow.
    So I will forgive because it is right,
    because, for both of us, it makes
    a better tomorrow.

Self-Love: Agape

God is Charity

And only when Charity arrives

Can those lesser loves,

Those lesser half-gods

Remain love, remain gods

And not rot until they are demons;

Devils that imprison the heart

In a cell as dark as Tartarus.

Or, without Charity, at best,

These lesser ones will just vanish.

But if they do, will even Charity

Still be what we know as Charity?

Are not these lesser loves

An inherent part of that one above

Them all, from which they come?

It is in the giving and reception of Charity

That all other loves, men, and beings

Live and move and have their being.[1]

It is agape that moves most implicitly

In each and every god and person's story.

---

[1] Acts 17:28

When one tries to love without Charity,

Even their love becomes a demon.

One must submit to that higher love

Or remain in their state, desolation.

Until the vision of judgment comes,

Until the silence overcomes the deafness,

Until one sees their chosen demons,

Admits their faults, realizes they are not

Right in the eyes of the ever just Charity,

They will know no forgiveness or pity.

But when they submit, Charity will permit

Them to walk through that eternal door

That was destined for them long before

Their first breath. Then they will hear and see

That all things must submit to Charity

Or they will never even be themselves.

Yes. All must bow to Charity, or else

Decay and be blown away, swept up

With time's winds, for their own, are none.

Every face is a gift of Charity's grace.

Above All

Silver. Gold. Fame. Power.

Cast them into the sea.

Let them sink. Let them sink.

Then let the One from Heaven

Come down to bring

The most prized possession

He can bring—a possession

No one has right to but He.

Let the One above all

Come and calm the seas.

With His word, He brings peace.

By the Word of God,

By the Word above all

Crucified on a tree,

He vanquishes sin's sting,

Then rises in victory,

Then spreads a gift in ascendancy.

What did He bring?
What did He give?
What did this One above all
Leave on earth in His ascent?
What is His most precious gift
That is no one's right but His?
It is the very thing that He is.

        1 John 4:8

For All

Against *such*, there is no law.
In *this*, you can do no wrong.
It is for mothers, brothers, sisters.
It is for friends, fathers, enemies.
It is for wives, daughters, neighbors.
It is for every great and small thing
On earth, above earth, beneath earth.
It is the source of abundant mirth.
It is the source of abundant pain.
It is the reason we bother at all
And can deal with hurt again and again.
No one can earn *it*. No one deserves *it*.
But *it* has been given freely to all
Who deny themselves and trust *it*.

The Call

Each and every person is unique.

There is no doubt about it.

We share much in common, certainly.

Still, we are all unique.

Our genes, our perspective, our history

Is our own. We claim it.

You are you. I am me.

No one lives inside another's body.

And most probably do not want to.

However, there is one piece

In every puzzling life that is not unique.

The cornerstone. The final piece

That holds it all together,

That makes the puzzle complete.

All share it and cannot escape it.

None can be guiltless in this decree,

This command that looms over humanity:

"Love one another as I have loved you."

A Prayer

Grey folds into black,
The haze of smog
Into a starless night.
Many souls—weary,
Wired, and anxious
—wait.

On either side
Of a barbed fence,
Between which lies
Bodies putrefied,
Are searching souls
Petrified:

In their hands, gripped,
Is an instrument meant
To bring death. Only death
—nothing else.

Yet, on each side,
With fervent affection,
One of these men
Is infected with
love.

I listen as each

Offers up a prayer,

One for the other

And all who will fall

Tonight

"Forgive them. They know not what they do."

I'll Meet God All the Way

I'll meet God all the way for you.

Whatever He requires, that I will do:

If it takes all I have, I will go.

If sweat drops like blood, I will go.

If every tear must be shed, I will go.

If hunger and thirst abound, I will go.

If I must walk myself into ground, I will go.

If I must climb high above Everest, I will go.

If I must crawl into the earth's crust, I will go.

If I should never be allowed to sleep, still, I will go.

If I should never be allowed to see light again, I will go.

If I must bear the weight of the world and its sin, I will go all the way.

I'll meet God all the way for you.

Whatever He requires, that I will do.

Whatever God wants me to,

I will do for Him, too.

Nature

Bees buzz. Birds chirp.

On hearing their symphonic toil,

I'm captured, taken away

Into a heavenly place.

Flowers bend in the wind.
Grass sways and trees creak.
I hear a tap-tap-tapping beat—
A mother bird's wings;
The woodpecker's beak:
Both, such curious things

I'm undone by nature's

Flood of colors and sounds.

By creation, I'm overwhelmed.

Music in every sound.

Art in every shape.

Beauty cannot be escaped.

It speaks of a better place.

It reminds the soul

That it has a home

Where beauty belongs.

Before I Was

Before I was, there was Love.
Before all were, there He was—
Love.

Before "Let there be light,"
Before "Let my people go,"
There Love was, living as One—
Father, Spirit, Son.

Before there was time,
Before the need of sacrifice,
He was Love.

Before there was even a speck of dust,
He reigned in life, He reigned as One,
In love, the perfect bond.

From always until always,
He remains the same,
He remains Love.

Made in the USA
Columbia, SC
27 June 2023